Painting with GIMP

By

U. C-Abel Books

TABLE OF CONTENTS

DEDICATION

We dedicate this book to all GIMP 2.8 users all over the world.

INTRODUCTION

Painting with GIMP is a compilation made to help painting artists do more in their field. It teaches them how to post results in a short while.

This book is part of the GIMP guide we compiled to help ourselves learn GNU Image Manipulation Program (GIMP) better, and as well have something we can run to when a challenge shows up. In sincerity, we never thought of selling this guide, or bringing it to the public at first until we saw how difficult the program was to people. So the purpose of this guide is not to extort money from readers, but to help them get better.

Whether you are doing painting as a profession or hobby, this book will help you a great deal.

Get in love with GIMP; manipulate your image in whatsoever manner that seems good to you.

Happy GIMPing!

Section 1: The Selection

Often when you operate on an image, you only want part of it to be affected. In GIMP, you make this happen by *selecting* that part. Each image has a *selection* associated with it. Most, but not all, GIMP operations act only on the selected portions of the image.

Figure 1.1. How would you isolate the tree?

There are many, many situations where creating just the right selection is the key to getting the result you want, and often it is not easy to do. For example, in the above image, suppose I want to cut the tree out from its background, and paste it into a different image. To do this, I need to create a selection that contains the tree and nothing but the tree. It is difficult because the tree has a complex shape, and in several spots is hard to distinguish from the objects behind it.

Figure 1.2. Selection shown as usual with dashed line.

Now here is a very important point, and it is crucial to understand this. Ordinarily when you create a selection, you see it as a dashed line enclosing a portion of the image. The common, not entirely accurate, idea you could get from this, is that the selection is a sort of container, with the selected parts of the image inside, and the unselected parts outside. Although this concept of selection is okay for many purposes, it is not entirely correct.

Actually the selection is implemented as a *channel*. In terms of its internal structure, it is identical to the red, green, blue, and alpha channels of an image. Thus, the selection has a value defined at each pixel of the image, ranging between 0 (unselected) and 255 (fully selected). The advantage of this approach is that it allows some pixels to be *partially selected*, by giving them intermediate values between 0 and 255. As you will see, there are many situations where it is desirable to have smooth transitions between selected and unselected regions.

What, then, is the dashed line that appears when you create a selection?

The dashed line is a *contour line*, dividing areas that are more than half selected from areas that are less than half selected.

Figure 1.3. Same selection in QuickMask mode.

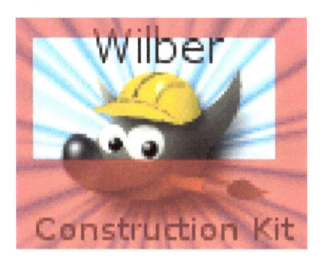

While looking at the dashed line that represents the selection, always remember that the line tells only part of the story. If you want to see the selection in complete detail, the easiest way is to click the QuickMask button in the lower left corner of the image window. This causes the selection to be shown as a translucent overlay atop the image. Selected areas are unaffected; unselected areas are reddened. The more completely selected an area is, the less red it appears.

Many operations work differently in QuickMask mode. Use the QuickMask button in the lower left corner of the image window to toggle QuickMask mode on and off.

Figure 1.4. Same selection in QuickMask mode after feathering.

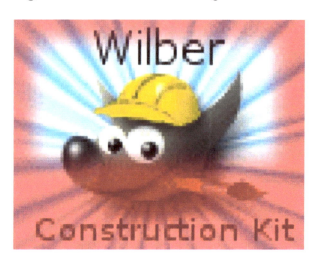

1.1. Feathering

With the default settings, the basic selection tools, such as the Rectangle Select tool, create sharp selections. Pixels inside the dashed line are fully selected, and pixels outside completely unselected. You can verify this by toggling QuickMask: you see a clear rectangle with sharp edges, surrounded by uniform red. Use the "Feather edges" checkbox in the Tool Options to toggle between graduated selections and sharp selections. The feather radius, which you can adjust, determines the distance over which the transition occurs.

If you are following along, try this with the Rectangle Select tool, and then toggle QuickMask. You will see that the clear rectangle has a fuzzy edge.

Feathering is particularly useful when you are cutting and pasting, so that the pasted object blends smoothly and unobtrusively with its surroundings.

It is possible to feather a selection at any time, even if it was originally created as a sharp selection. Use Select → Feather from the image menu to open the Feather Selection dialog. Set the feather radius and click OK. Use Select → Sharpen to do the opposite—sharpen a graduated selection into an all-or-nothing selection.

 Note

For technically oriented readers: feathering works by applying a Gaussian blur to the selection channel, with the specified blurring radius.

1.2. Making a Selection Partially Transparent

You can set layer opacity, but you cannot do that directly for a selection. It is quite useful to make the image of a glass transparent. Use the following methods to set the layer opacity:

- For simple selections, use the Eraser tool with the desired opacity.
- For complex selections: use Selection → Floating to create a floating selection. This creates a new layer with the selection called "Floating Selection". Set the opacity slider in the Layer Dialog to the desired opacity. Then anchor the selection: outside the selection, the mouse pointer includes an anchor. When you click while the mouse pointer includes the anchor, the floating selection disappears from the Layer Dialog and the selection is at the right place and partially transparent (anchoring works this way only if a selection tool is activated: you can also use the Anchor Layer command in the context menu by right clicking on the selected layer in the layer dialog).

  And, if you use this function frequently: **Ctrl-C** to copy the selection, **Ctrl-V** to paste the clipboard as a floating selection, and Layer → New Layer to turn the selection into a new layer. You can adjust the opacity before, or after creating the new layer.

- Another way: use Layer → Mask → Add Layer Mask to add a layer mask to the layer with the selection, initializing it with the selection. Then use a brush with the desired opacity to paint the selection with black, i.e. paint it with transparency. Then Layer/Mask/Apply Layer Mask.

- To *make the solid background of an image transparent*, add an Alpha channel, and use the Magic Wand to select the background. Then, use the Color Picker tool to select the background color, which becomes the foreground color in Toolbox. Use the Bucket Fill tool with the selected color. Set the Bucket Fill mode to "Color Erase", which erases pixels with the selected color; other pixels are partially erased and their color is changed.

The simplest method is to use Edit $\rightarrow$ Clear, which gives complete transparency to a selection.

Section 2: Creating and Using Selections.

2.1. Moving a Selection

Rectangular and elliptical selections have two modes. The default mode has handles on the selection. If you click the selection or press the **Enter** key, the handles disappear leaving only the dotted outline (marching ants). The other selection tools have different behaviour.

2.1.1. Moving rectangular and elliptical selections

If you click-and drag a selection with handles, you move the selection outline, and you don't move the contents of rectangular or elliptic selections.

Select the **Move** tool and set the options to move the selection; the tool supports moving the selection, path, or layer.

Figure 1.5. Moving selection outline

Most systems support moving the selection using the arrow keys. The precise behavior is system dependent. If the arrow keys do not cause the selection to move, try hovering the mouse cursor over the selection first. Press and hold the **Alt** (or **Ctrl**+**Alt**, **Shift**+**Alt**, or **Alt**). One combination may move the selection by one pixel, and another by 25 pixels each step. Hover the mouse cursor over a side or corner handle, and the arrow keys and combinations can change the size of the selection.

If you click-and-drag the selection without handles, you create a new selection! To move the selection contents, you have to

13

- hold down **Ctrl**+**Alt** keys and click-and-drag the selection. This makes the original place empty. A floating selection is created. The required key commands may differ on your system, look in the status bar to see if another combination is specified; for example, **Shift**+**Ctrl**+**Alt**.

Figure 1.6. Moving a selection and its content, emptying the original place

- hold down **Shift**+**Alt** keys and click-and-drag the selection to move without emptying the original place. A floating selection is created.

Figure 1.7. Moving a selection and its content without emptying the original place

 Note

On some systems, you must push **Alt** before **Shift** or **Ctrl**. On these systems, pressing **Shift** or **Ctrl** first, causes GIMP to enter a mode that adds or subtract from the current selection — after that, the **Alt** key is ineffective!

2.1.2. Moving the other selections

The other selections (Lasso, Magic wand, By Color) have no handle. Click-and dragging them doesn't move them. To move their contents, as with rectangular and elliptical selections, you have to hold down **Ctrl**+**Alt** keys or **Shift**+**Alt** and click-and-drag.

If you use keyboard arrow keys instead of click-and-drag, you move the outline.

2.1.3. Other method

 Note

You can also use a more roundabout method to move a selection. Make it floating. Then you can move its content, emptying the origin, by click-and-dragging or keyboard arrow keys. To move without emptying, use copy-paste.

2.2. Adding or subtracting selections

Tools have options that you can configure. Each selection tool allows you to set the selection mode. The following selection modes are supported:

- Replace is the most used selection mode. In replace mode, a selection replaces any existing selection.
- Add mode, causes new selections to be added to any existing selection. Press and hold the **Shift** key while making a selection to temporarily enter add mode.
- Subtract mode, causes new selections to be removed from any existing selection. Press and hold the **Ctrl** key while making a selection to temporarily enter subtract mode.
- Intersect mode, causes areas in both the new and existing selection to become the new selection. Press and hold both the **Shift** and **Ctrl** key while making a selection to temporarily enter intersect mode.

Figure 1.8. Enlarging a rectangular selection with the Lasso

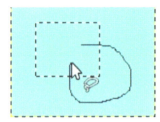 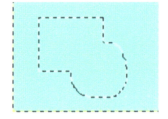

The figure shows an existing rectangular selection. Select the Lasso. While pressing the **Shift** key, make a free hand selection that includes the existing selection. Release the mouse button and areas are included in the selection.

 Note

To correct selection defects precisely, use the **Quick Mask**.

Section 3: The QuickMask

Figure 1.9. Image with QuickMask enabled

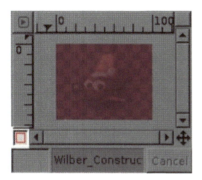

The usual **selection tools** involve tracing an outline around an area of interest, which does not work well for some complex selections. The QuickMask, however, allows you to paint a selection instead of just tracing its outline.

3.1. Overview

Normally, a selection in GIMP is represented by "marching ants" that trace the selection outline, but there may be more to a selection than the marching ants show. A GIMP selection is actually a full-fledged grayscale channel, covering the image, with pixel values ranging from 0 (unselected) to 255 (fully selected). The marching ants are drawn along a contour of half-selected pixels. Thus, what the marching ants show you as either inside or outside the boundary is really just a slice through a continuum.

The QuickMask is GIMP's way of showing the full structure of the selection. QuickMask also provides the ability to interact with the selection in new, and substantially more powerful, ways. Click the small outlined button at the lower left of the image window to toggle QuickMask on and off. The button switches between QuickMask mode, and marching ants mode. You can also use Select → Toggle QuickMask, or **Shift**+**Q**, to toggle between QuickMask and marching ants mode.

In QuickMask mode, the selection is shown as a translucent screen overlying the image, whose transparency at each pixel indicates the degree to which that pixel is selected. By default the mask is shown in red, but you can change this if another mask color is more convenient. The less a pixel is selected, the more it is obscured by the mask. Fully selected pixels are shown completely clear.

In QuickMask mode, many image manipulations act on the selection channel rather than the image itself. This includes, in particular, paint tools. Painting with white selects pixels, and painting with black unselects pixels. You can use any of the paint tools, as well as the bucket fill and gradient fill tools, in this way. Advanced users of GIMP learn that "painting the selection" is the easiest and most effective way to delicately manipulate the image.

Tip

To save a QuickMask selection to a new channel; Make sure that there is a selection and that QuickMask mode is not active in the image window. Use Select → Save to Channel. to create a new channel in the channel dialog called "SelectionMask copy" (repeating this command creates "..copy#1", "...copy#2" and so on...).

Tip

In QuickMask mode, Cut and Paste act on the selection rather than the image. You can sometimes make use of this as the most convenient way of transferring a selection from one image to another.

You can learn more on Selection masks in the section dedicated to the channel dialog.

3.2. Properties

There are two QuickMask properties you can change by right-clicking on the QuickMask button.

- Normally the QuickMask shows unselected areas "fogged over" and selected areas "in clear", but you can reverse this by choosing "Mask Selected Areas" instead of the default "Mask Unselected Areas".
- Use "Configure Color and Opacity" to open a dialog that allows you to set these to values other than the defaults, which are red at 50% opacity.

Section 4: Using QuickMask Mode

1. Open an image or begin a new document.
2. Activate QuickMask mode using the left-bottom button in the image window. If a selection is present the mask is initialized with the content of the selection.
3. Choose any drawing tool. Paint on the QuickMask with black to remove selected areas, and paint with white to add selected areas. Use grey colors to partially select areas.

   You can also use selection tools and fill these selections with the Bucket Fill tool; this does not destroy the QuickMask selections!

4. Toggle QuickMask mode off using the left-bottom button in the image window: the selection will be displayed with marching ants.

Section 5: Paths

Paths are curves (known as Bézier-curves). Paths are easy to learn and use in GIMP. To understand their concepts and mechanism, look at the glossary Bézier-curve or Wikipedia WKPD-BEZIER. The Paths tool is very powerful, allowing you to design sophisticated forms. To use the Paths tool in GIMP, you must first create a path, and then stroke the path.

In GIMP, the term "Stroke path" means to apply a specific style to the path (color, width, pattern...).

A Path has two main purposes:

- You can convert a closed path to a selection.
- Any path, open or closed, can be *stroked*; that is, painted on the image in a variety of ways.

Figure 1.10. Illustration of four different path creating

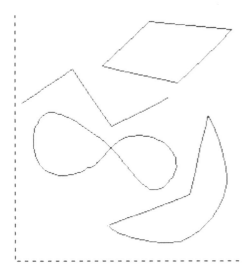

Four examples of GIMP paths: one closed and polygonal; one open and polygonal; one closed and curved; one with a mixture of straight and curved segments.

5.1. Path Creation

Start by drawing the outline for your path; the outline can be modified later (see the **Paths** tool). To start, select the Paths tool using one of the following methods:

- Use Tools → Path from the image menu.
- Use the relevant icon in toolbox.
- Use the hotkey **B**.

When the Paths tool is selected, the mouse cursor changes into a pointer (arrow) with a curve. Left click in the image to create the first point on the path. Move the mouse to a new point and left click the mouse to create another point linked to the previous point. Although you can create as many points as you desire, you only need two points to learn about Paths. While adding points, the mouse cursor has a little "+" next to the curve, which indicates that clicking will add a new point. When the mouse cursor is close to a line segment, the "+" changes into a cross with arrows; like the move tool.

Move the mouse cursor close to a line segment, left-click and drag the line segment. Two events occur.

- The line segment bends and curves as it is pulled.
- Each line segment has a start point and an end point that is clearly labeled. A "direction line" now projects from each end point for the line segment that was moved.

The curved line segment leaves an end point in the same direction that the "direction line" leaves the end point. The length of the "direction line" controls how far the line segment projects along the "direction line" before curving toward the other end point. Each "direction line" has an empty square box (called a handle) on one end. Click and drag a handle to change the direction and length of a "direction line".

Figure 1.11. Appearance of a path while it is manipulated

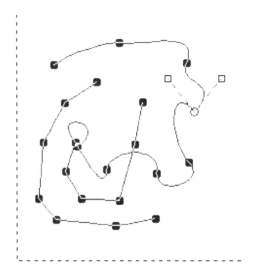

Appearance of a path while it is manipulated using the Path tool.

The path is comprised of two components with both straight and curved segments. Black squares are anchor points, the open circle indicates the selected anchor, and the two open squares are the handles associated with the selected anchor.

5.2. Path Properties

Paths, like layers and channels, are components of an image. When an image is saved in GIMP's native XCF file format, any paths it has are saved with it. The list of paths in an image can be viewed and operated on using the **Paths dialog.** You can move a path from one image to another by copying and pasting using the pop-up menu in the Paths dialog, or by dragging an icon from the Paths dialog into the destination image window.

GIMP paths belong to a mathematical type called "Bezier paths". What this means in practical terms is that they are defined by *anchors* and *handles*. "Anchors" are points the path goes through. "Handles" define the direction of a path when it enters or leaves an anchor point: each anchor point has two handles attached to it.

Paths can be very complex. If you create them by hand using the Path tool, unless you are obsessive they probably won't contain more than a few dozen anchor points (often many fewer); but if you create them by transforming a selection into a path, or by transforming text into a path, the result can easily contain hundreds of anchor points, or even thousands.

A path may contain multiple *components*. A "component" is a part of a path whose anchor points are all connected to each other by path segments. The ability to have multiple components in paths allows you to convert them into selections having multiple disconnected parts.

Each component of a path can be either *open* or *closed*: "closed" means that the last anchor point is connected to the first anchor point. If you transform a path into a selection, any open components are automatically converted into closed components by connecting the last anchor point to the first anchor point with a straight line.

Path segments can be either straight or curved. A path is called "polygonal" if all of its segments are straight. A new path segment is always created straight; the handles for the anchor points are directly on top of the anchor points, yielding handles of zero length, which produces straight-line segments. Drag a handle away from an anchor point to cause a segment to curve.

One nice thing about paths is that they use very few resources, especially in comparison with images. Representing a path in RAM requires storing only the coordinates of its anchors and handles: 1K of memory is enough to hold a complex path, but not enough to hold a small 20x20 pixel RGB layer. Therefore, it is possible to have literally hundreds of paths in an image without causing any significant stress to your system; the amount of stress that hundreds of paths might cause *you*, however, is another question. Even a path with thousands of segments consumes minimal resources in comparison to a typical layer or channel.

Paths can be created and manipulated using the **Path tool.**

24

5.3. Paths and Selections

GIMP lets you transform the selection for an image into a path; it also lets you transform paths into selections.

When you transform a selection into a path, the path closely follows the "marching ants". Now, the selection is a two-dimensional entity, but a path is a one-dimensional entity, so there is no way to transform the selection into a path without losing information. In fact, any information about partially selected areas (i.e., feathering) are lost when a selection is turned into a path. If the path is transformed back into a selection, the result is an all-or-none selection, similar to what is obtained by executing "Sharpen" from the Select menu.

5.4. Transforming Paths

Each of the Transform tools (Rotate, Scale, Perspective, etc) can be set to act on a layer, selection, or path. Select the transform tool in the toolbox, then select layer, selection, or path for the "Transform:" option in the tool's Tool Options dialog. This gives you a powerful set of methods for altering the shapes of paths without affecting other elements of the image.

By default a Transform tool, when it is set to affect paths, acts on only one path: the *active path* for the image, which is shown highlighted in the Paths dialog. You can make a transformation affect more than one path, and possibly other things as well, using the "transform lock" buttons in the Paths dialog. Not only paths, but also layers and channels, can be transform-locked. If you transform one element that is transform-locked, all others will be transformed in the same way. So, for example, if you want to scale a layer and a path by the same amount, click the transform-lock buttons so that "chain" symbols appear next to the layer in the Layers dialog, and the path in the Paths dialog; then use the Scale tool on either the layer or the path, and the other will automatically follow.

Figure 1.12. Stroking paths

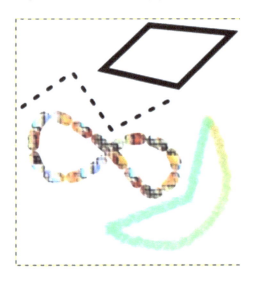

The four paths from the top illustration, each stroked in a different way.

Paths do not alter the appearance of the image pixel data unless they are *stroked*, using Edit → Stroke Path from the image menu or the Paths dialog right-click menu, or the "Stroke Path" button in the Tool Options dialog for the Path tool.

Choosing "Stroke Path" by any of these means brings up a dialog that allows you to control the way the stroking is done. You can choose from a wide variety of line styles, or you can stroke with any of the Paint tools, including unusual ones such as the Clone tool, Smudge tool, Eraser, etc.

1.13. The Stroke Path dialog

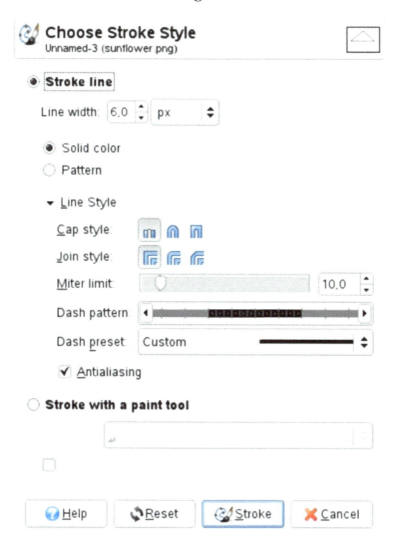

You can further increase the range of stroking effects by stroking a path multiple times, or by using lines or brushes of different widths. The possibilities for getting interesting effects in this way are almost unlimited.

5.6. Paths and Text

Figure 1.14. Text converted to a path

Text converted to a path
and then transformed
using the Perspective tool.

The path shown above, stroked with
a fuzzy brush and then gradient-mapped
using the Gradient Map filter with the "
Yellow Contrast" gradient.

The path shown above, stroked with a fuzzy brush and then gradient-mapped using the Gradient Map filter with the "Yellow Contrast" gradient.

A text item created using the Text tool can be transformed into a path using the **Path from Text** command in the context menu of the Text tool. This can be useful for several purposes, including:

- Stroking the path, which gives you many possibilities for fancy text.
- More importantly, transforming the text. Converting text into a path, then transforming the path, and finally either stroking the path or converting it to a selection and filling it, often leads to much higher-quality results than rendering the text as a layer and transforming the pixel data.

5.7. Paths and SVG files

SVG, standing for "Scalable Vector Graphics", is an increasingly popular file format for *vector graphics*, in which graphical elements are represented in a resolution-independent format, in contrast to *raster graphics*; in which graphical elements are represented as arrays of pixels. GIMP is mainly a raster graphics program, but paths are vector entities.

Fortunately, paths are represented in SVG files in almost exactly the same way they are represented in GIMP. (Actually fortune has nothing to do with it: GIMP's path handling was rewritten for GIMP 2.0 with SVG paths in mind.) This compatibility makes it possible to store GIMP paths as SVG files without losing any information. You can access this capability in the Paths dialog.

It also means that GIMP can create paths from SVG files saved in other programs, such as Inkscape or Sodipodi, two popular open-source vector graphics applications. This is nice because those programs have much more powerful path-manipulation tools than GIMP does. You can import a path from an SVG file using the Paths dialog.

The SVG format handles many other graphical elements than just paths: among other things, it handles figures such as squares, rectangles, circles, ellipses, regular polygons, etc. GIMP cannot do anything with these entities, but it can load them as paths.

Section 6: Brushes

Figure 1.15. Brush strokes example

A number of examples of brushstrokes painted using different brushes from the set supplied with GIMP. All were painted using the Paintbrush tool.

A *brush* is a pixmap or set of pixmaps used for painting. GIMP includes a set of 10 "paint tools", which not only perform operations that you would normally think of as painting, but also operations such as erasing, copying, smudging, lightening or darkening, etc. All of the paint tools, except the ink tool, use the same set of brushes. The brush pixmaps represent the marks that are made by single "touches" of the brush to the image. A brush stroke, usually made by moving the pointer across the image with the mouse button held down, produces a series of marks spaced along the trajectory, in a way specified by the characteristics of the brush and the paint tool being used.

Brushes can be selected by clicking on an icon in the **Brushes dialog**. GIMP's *current brush* is shown in the Brush/Pattern/Gradient area of the Toolbox. Clicking on the brush symbol there is one way of activating the Brushes dialog.

When you install GIMP, it comes with a number of basic brushes, plus a few bizarre ones that serve mainly to give you examples of what is possible (i. e., the "green pepper" brush in the illustration). You can also create new brushes, or download them and install them so that GIMP will recognize them.

GIMP can use several different types of brushes. All of them, however, are used in the same way, and for most purposes you don't need to worry about the differences when you paint with them. Here are the available types of brushes:

Ordinary brushes

> Most of the brushes supplied with GIMP fall into this category. They are represented in the Brushes dialog by grayscale pixmaps. When you paint using them, the current foreground color (as shown in the Color Area of the Toolbox) is substituted for black, and the pixmap shown in the brushes dialog represents the mark that the brush makes on the image.

> To create such a brush: Create a small image in gray levels using zoom. Save it with the .gbr extension. Click on Refresh button in the Brush Dialog to get it in preview without it being necessary to restart GIMP.

Color brushes

> Brushes in this category are represented by colored images in the Brushes dialog. They can be pictures or text. When you paint with them, the colors are used as shown; the current foreground color does not come into play. Otherwise they work the same way as ordinary brushes.

To create such a brush: Create a small RGBA image. For this, open New Image, select RGB for image type and Transparent for fill type. Draw your image and firs save it as a .xcf file to keep its properties. Then save it in *.gbr* format. Click on the *Refresh* button in Brush Dialog to get your brush without it being necessary to restart GIMP.

Tip

When you do a Copy or a Cut on a selection, you see the contents of the clipboard (that is the selection) at the first position in the brushes dialog. And you can use it for painting.

Figure 1.16. Selection to Brush after Copy or Cut

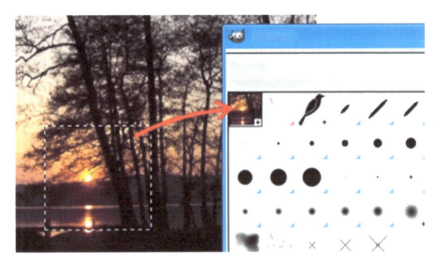

Image hoses / Image pipes

Brushes in this category can make more than one kind of mark on an image. They are indicated by small red triangles at the lower right corner of the brush symbol in the Brushes dialog. They are sometimes called "animated brushes" because the marks change as you trace out a brushstroke. In principle, image hose brushes can be very sophisticated, especially if you use a tablet, changing shape as a function of pressure, angle, etc. These possibilities have never really been exploited, however; and the ones supplied with GIMP are relatively simple (but still quite useful).

You will find an example on how to create such brushes in **Animated brushes.**

Parametric brushes

These are brushes created using the **Brush Editor**, which allows you to generate a wide variety of brush shapes by using a simple graphical interface. A nice feature of parametric brushes is that they are *resizable*. It is possible, using the Preferences dialog, to make key presses or mouse wheel rotations cause the current brush to become larger or smaller, if it is a parametric brush.

Now, all brushes have a variable size. In fact, in the option box of all painting tools there is a slider to enlarge or reduce the size of the active brush. You can do this directly in the image window if you have set correctly your mouse wheel; see **Varying Brush Size** at **Page 47.**

In addition to the brush pixmap, each GIMP brush has one other important property: the brush *Spacing*. This represents the distance between consecutive brush-marks when a continuous brushstroke is painted. Each brush has an assigned default value for this, which can be modified using the Brushes dialog.

Section 7: Adding New Brushes

To add a new brush, after either creating or downloading it, you need to save it in a format GIMP can use. The brush file needs to be placed in the GIMP's brush search path, so that GIMP is able to index and display it in the Brushes dialog. You can hit the Refresh button, which reindexes the brush directory. GIMP uses three file formats for brushes:

GBR

> The .gbr ("gimp *br*ush") format is used for ordinary and color brushes. You can convert many other types of images, including many brushes used by other programs, into GIMP brushes by opening them in GIMP and saving them with file names ending in .gbr. This brings up a dialog box in which you can set the default Spacing for the brush. A more complete description of the GBR file format can be found in the file gbr.txt in the devel-docs directory of the GIMP source distribution.

> **Figure 1.17. Save a .gbr brush**

GIH

> The .gih ("gimp *i*mage *h*ose") format is used for animated brushes. These brushes are constructed from images containing

34

multiple layers: each layer may contain multiple brush-shapes, arranged in a grid. When you save an image as a .gih file, a dialog comes up that allows you to describe the format of the brush. Look at **The GIH dialog box** for more information about the dialog. The GIH format is rather complicated: a complete description can be found in the file gih.txt in the devel-docs directory of the GIMP source distribution.

VBR

The .vbr format is used for parametric brushes, i.e., brushes created using the Brush Editor. There is really no other meaningful way of obtaining files in this format.

To make a brush available, place it in one of the folders in GIMP's brush search path. By default, the brush search path includes two folders, the system brushes folder, which you should not use or alter, and the brushes folder inside your personal GIMP directory. You can add new folders to the brush search path using the **Brush Folders** page of the Preferences dialog. Any GBR, GIH, or VBR file included in a folder in the brush search path will show up in the Brushes dialog the next time you start GIMP, or as soon as you press the Refresh button in the Brushes dialog.

 Note

When you create a new parametric brush using the Brush Editor, it is automatically saved in your personal brushes folder.

There are a number of web sites with downloadable collections of GIMP brushes. Rather than supplying a list of links that will soon be out of date, the best advice is to do a search with your favorite search engine for "GIMP brushes". There are also many collections of brushes for other programs with painting functionality. Some can be converted easily into GIMP brushes, some require special conversion utilities, and some cannot be converted at all. Most fancy procedural brush types fall into the last category. If you need to know, look around on the web, and if you don't find anything, look for an expert to ask.

Section 8: The GIH Dialog Box

When your new animated brush is created, it is displayed within the image window and you would like save it into a gih format. You select File → Save as... menu, name your work with the gih extension in the new window relevant field and as soon as you pressed the Save button, the following window is displayed:

Figure 1.18. The dialog to describe the animated brush

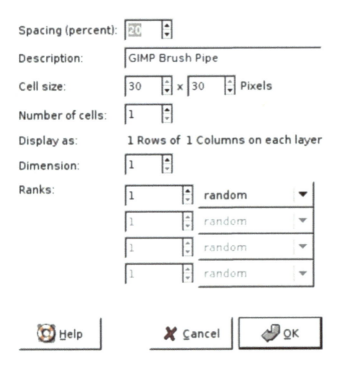

This dialog box shows up, if you save an image as GIMP image hose

This dialog box has several options not easy to understand. They allow you to determine the way your brush is animated.

Spacing (Percent)

"Spacing" is the distance between consecutive brush marks when you trace out a brushstroke with the pointer. You must consider drawing with a brush, whatever the paint tool, like stamping. If Spacing is low, stamps will be very close and stroke look continuous. If spacing is high, stamps will be separated: that's interesting with a color brush (like "green pepper" for instance). Value varies from 1 to 200 and this percentage refers to brush "diameter": 100% is one diameter.

Description

It's the brush name that will appear at the top of Brush Dialog (grid mode) when the brush is selected.

Cell Size

That's size of cells you will cut up in layers... Default is one cell per layer and size is that of the layer. Then there is only one brush aspect per layer.

We could have only one big layer and cut up in it the cells that will be used for the different aspects of the animated brush.

For instance, we want a 100x100 pixels brush with 8 different aspects. We can take these 8 aspects from a 400x200 pixels layer, or from a 300x300 pixels layer but with one cell unused.

Number of cells

That's the number of cells (one cell per aspect) that will be cut in every layer. Default is the number of layers as there is only one layer per aspect.

Display as

This tells how cells have been arranged in layers. If, for example, you have placed height cells at the rate of two cells per layer on four layers, GIMP will display: 1 rows of 2 columns on each layer.

There things are getting complicated! Explanations are necessary to understand how to arrange cell and layers.

GIMP starts retrieving cells from each layer and stacks them into a FIFO stack (First In First Out: the first in is at the top of the stack and so can be first out). In our example 4 layers with 2 cells in each, we'll have, from top to bottom: first cell of first layer, second cell of first layer, first cell of second layer, second cell of second layer..., second cell of fourth layer. With one cell per layer or with several cells per layer, result is the same. You can see this stack in the Layer Dialog of the resulting .gih image file.

Then GIMP creates a computer array from this stack with the Dimensions you have set. You can use four dimensions.

In computer science an array has a "myarray(x,y,z)" form for a 3 dimensions array (3D). It's easy to imagine a 2D array: on a paper it's an array with rows and columns

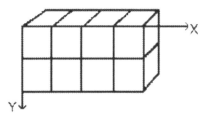

With a 3d array we don't talk rows and columns but Dimensions and Ranks. The first dimension is along x axis, the second dimension along y axis, the third along z axis. Each dimension has ranks of cells.

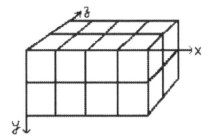

To fill up this array, GIMP starts retrieving cells from the top of stack. The way it fills the array reminds that of an odometer: right rank digits turn first and, when they reach their maximum, left rank digits start running. If you have some memories of Basic programming you will have, with an array(4,2,2), the following succession:
(1,1,1),(1,1,2),(1,2,1),(1,2,2),(2,1,1),(2,1,2),(2,2,2),(3,1,1)....
(4,2,2). We will see this later in an example.

Besides the rank number that you can give to each dimension, you can also give them a Selection mode. You have several modes that will be applied when drawing:

Incremental

GIMP selects a rank from the concerned dimension according to the order ranks have in that dimension.

Random

GIMP selects a rank at random from the concerned dimension.

Angular

GIMP selects a rank in the concerned dimension according to the moving angle of the brush.

The first rank is for the direction 0°, upwards. The other ranks are affected, clockwise, to an angle whose value is 360/number of ranks. So, with 4 ranks in the concerned dimension, the angle will move 90° clockwise for each direction change: second rank will be affected to 90° (rightwards), third rank to 180° (downwards) and fourth rank to 270° (-90°) (leftwards).[2]

Speed, Pressure, x tilt, y tilt

These options are for sophisticated drawing tablets.

Examples

A one dimension image pipe

Well! What is all this useful for? We'll see that gradually with examples. You can actually place in each dimension cases that will give your brush a particular action.

Let us start with a 1D brush which will allow us to study selection modes action. We can imagine it like this:

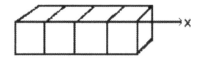

Follow these steps:

1. Open a new 30x30 pixels image, RGB with Transparent fill type. Using the Text tool create 4 layers "1", "2", "3", "4". Delete the "background" layer.
2. Save this image first with .xcf extension to keep its properties then save it as .gih.
3. The Save As Dialog is opened: select a destination for your image. OK. The GIH dialog is opened: Choose Spacing 100, give a name in Description box, 30x30 for Cell Size, 1 dimension, 4 ranks and choose "Incremental" in Selection box. OK.
4. You may have difficulties to save directly in the GIMP Brush directory. In that case, save the .gih file manually into the /usr/share/gimp/gimp/2.0/brushes directory. Then

come back into the Toolbox, click in the brush icon to open the Brush Dialog then click on Refresh ↻icon button. Your new brush appears in the Brush window. Select it. Select pencil tool for instance and click and hold with it on a new image:

You see 1, 2, 3, 4 digits following one another in order.

5. Take your .xcf image file back and save it as .gih setting Selection to "Random":

Digits will be displayed at random order.

6. Now select "Angular" Selection:

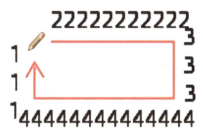

A 3 dimensions image hose

We are now going to create a 3D animated brush: its orientation will vary according to brush direction, it will alternate Left/Right hands regularly and its color will vary at random between black and blue.

The first question we have to answer to is the number of images that is necessary. We reserve the first dimension (x) to the brush direction (4 directions). The second dimension (y) is for Left/Right alternation and the third dimension (z) for color variation. Such a brush is represented in a 3D array "myarray(4,2,2)":

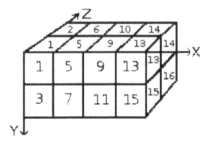

There are 4 ranks in first dimension (x), 2 ranks in second dimension (y) and 2 ranks in third dimension (z). We see that there are 4x2x2 = 16 cells. We need 16 images.

1. **Creating images of dimension 1 (x)**

   Open a new 30x30 pixels image, RGB with Transparent Fill Type. Using the zoom draw a left hand with fingers upwards.[3] Save it as handL0k.xcf (hand Left 0° Black).

   Open the Layer Dialog. Double click on the layer to open the Layer Attributes Dialog and rename it to handL0k.

   Duplicate the layer. Let visible only the duplicated layer, select it and apply a 90° rotation (Layer/Transform/ 90° rotation clockwise). Rename it to handL90k.

   Repeat the same operations to create handL180k and handL-90k (or handL270k).

2. **Creating images of dimension 2 (y)**

   This dimension in our example has two ranks, one for left hand and the other for right hand. The left hand rank exists yet. We shall build right hand images by flipping it horizontally.

Duplicate the handL0k layer. Let it visible only and select it. Rename it to handR0K. Apply Layer/Transform/Flip Horizontally.

Repeat the same operation on the other left hand layers to create their right hand equivalent.

Re-order layers to have a clockwise rotation from top to bottom, alternating Left and Right: handL0k, handR0k, handL90k, handR90k, ..., handR-90k.

3. **Creating images of dimension 3 (z)**

Creating images of dimension 3 (z): The third dimension has two ranks, one for black color and the other for blue color. The first rank, black, exists yet. We will see that images of dimension 3 will be a copy, in blue, of the images of dimension 2. So we will have our 16 images. But a row of 16 layers is not easy to manage: we will use layers with two images.

Select the handL0k layer and let it visible only. Using Image/Canvas Size change canvas size to 60x30 pixels.

Duplicate hand0k layer. On the copy, fill the hand with blue using Bucket Fill tool.

Now, select the Move tool. Double click on it to accede to its properties: check Move the Current Layer option. Move the blue hand into the right part of the layer precisely with the help of Zoom.

Make sure only handL0k and its blue copy are visible. Right click on the Layer Dialog: Apply the Merge Visible

Layers command with the option Expand as Necessary. You get a 60x30 pixels layer with the black hand on the left and the blue hand on the right. Rename it to "handsL0".

Repeat the same operations on the other layers.

4. Set layers in order

Layers must be set in order so that GIMP can find the required image at some point of using the brush. Our layers are yet in order but we must understand more generally how to have them in order. There are two ways to imagine this setting in order. The first method is mathematical: GIMP divides the 16 layers first by 4; that gives 4 groups of 4 layers for the first dimension. Each group represents a direction of the brush. Then, it divides each group by 2; that gives 8 groups of 2 layers for the second dimension: each group represents a L/R alternation. Then another division by 2 for the third dimension to represent a color at random between black and blue.

The other method is visual, by using the array representation. Correlation between two methods is represented in next image:

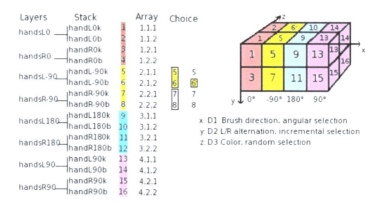

44

How will GIMP read this array?: GIMP starts with the first dimension which is programmed for "angular", for instance 90°. In this 90° rank, in yellow, in the second dimension, it selects a L/R alternation, in an "incremental" way. Then, in the third dimension, in a random way, it chooses a color. Finally, our layers must be in the following order:

5. Voilà. Your brush is ready. Save it as .xcf first, then as .gih with the following parameters:
   - Spacing: 100
   - Description: Hands
   - Cell Size: 30x30
   - Number of cells: 16
   - Dimensions: 3
     - Dimension 1: 4 ranks Selection: Angular
     - Dimension 2: 2 ranks Selection: Incremental
     - Dimension 3: 2 ranks Selection: Random

Place your .gih file into GIMP brush directory and refresh the brush box. You can now use your brush.

Figure 1.19. Here is the result by stroking an elliptical selection with the brush:

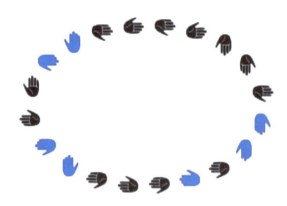

This brush alternates right hand and left hand regularly, black and blue color at random, direction according to four brush directions.

For previous GIMP versions you may have to replace "clockwise" with "counter-clockwise".

Section 9: Varying brush size

From GIMP-2.4, all brushes have a variable size.

9.1. How to vary the height of a brush

You can get the brush size varying in three ways:

1. Using the Scale slider of the tool that uses the brush. Pencil, Paintbrush, Eraser, Airbrush, Clone, Heal, Perspective Clone, Blur/Sharpen and Dodge/Burn tools have a slider to vary brush size.

   Figure 1.20. The Scale slider

   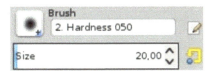

2. By programming the mouse wheel:
   1. In the main window of GIMP, click on Edit → Preferences.
   2. In the left column of the new window, select Input Devices → Input Controllers.
   3. You can see Additional Input Controllers, with two columns: Available Controllers and Active Controllers.

      In the column Active Controllers, double-click the Main Mouse Wheel button.

   4. Then, you see a new window: Configure Input Controller.

      In the left column Event, click Scroll Up to get it highlighted.

   5. Click the Edit button (at the bottom middle of the list).

6. You can see the window Select Controller Event Action.

   Drop-down the Tools item, by clicking the small triangle on its left.

7. In the left column Action, click Increase Brush Scale to highlight it, then click the OK button.
8. Now, in front of Scroll Up is display tools-paint-brush-scale-increase.
9. Close the window.
10. With the same method, program Scroll Down with Decrease Brush Scale.
11. Don't forget to click the OK button of the main window of Preferences.

After these somewhat long explanations, you can use your mouse wheel to vary size brush. For example, choose the pencil tool with the "Circle" brush. Set the pointer in the image window, use the mouse wheel, in the two directions, you can see the "Circle" shrinking or stretching.

3. You can program the "Up" and "Down" arrow keys of the keyboard.

The method is similar to that of the mouse wheel. The only differences are:

- In the column Active Controllers, double-click Main Keyboard.
- In the column Event, click Cursor Up for the first key, and Cursor Down for the second key.
- Then, use the two keys (Up arrow and Down arrow) and the result is the same as you got with the mouse wheel.

9.2. Creating a brush quickly

Two methods to create a new brush easily:

1. First, the "superfast" method. You have an image area you want make a brush from it, to be used with a tool like pencil, airbrush... Select it with the rectangular (or elliptical) select tool, then do a Copy of this selection and immediately you can see this copy in the first position of the Brush Dialog, and its name is "Clipboard". It is immediately usable.

Figure 1.21. Selection becomes a brush after copying

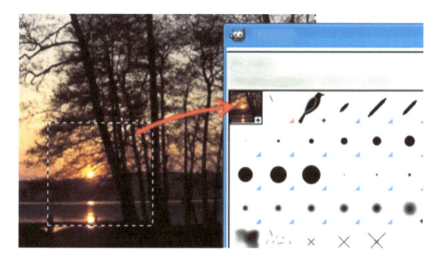

2. The second method is more elaborate.

   Do File → New with, for example, a width and a length of 35 pixels and in the advanced options a Color Space in Gray Level and Fill with: white.

   Zoom on this new image to enlarge it and draw on it with a black pencil.

   Save it with a .gbr extension in the directory /home/name_of_user/.gimp-2.8/brushes/.

   In the Brushes dialog window, click on the button Refresh brushes ⟳ And your marvellous brush appears right in the middle of the other brushes. You can use it immediately, without starting GIMP again.

Figure 1.22. Steps to create a brush

Draw images,
save as brush

Refresh brushes

Use the brush

Section 10: Gradients

Figure 1.23. Some examples of GIMP gradients.

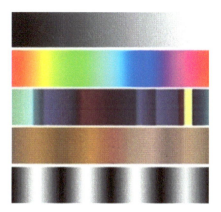

Gradients from top to bottom: FG to BG (RGB); Full saturation spectrum; Nauseating headache; Browns; Four bars

A *gradient* is a set of colors arranged in a linear order. The most basic use of gradients is by the **Blend tool**, sometimes known as the "gradient tool" or "gradient fill tool": it works by filling the selection with colors from a gradient. You have many options to choose from for controlling the way the gradient colors are arranged within the selection. There are also other important ways to use gradients, including:

Painting with a gradient

> Each of GIMP's basic painting tools allows you the option of using colors from a gradient. This enables you to create brushstrokes that change color from one end to the other.

The Gradient Map filter

This filter is now in the Colors menu, and allows you to "colorize" an image, using the color intensity of each point with the corresponding color from the active gradient (the intensity 0, very dark, is replaced by the color at most left end of the gradient, progressively until the intensity is 255, very light, replaced by the most right color of the gradient.

When you install GIMP, it comes presupplied with a large number of interesting gradients, and you can add new ones that you create or download from other sources. You can access the full set of available gradients using the **Gradients dialog,** a dockable dialog that you can either activate when you need it, or keep around as a tab in a dock. The "current gradient", used in most gradient-related operations, is shown in the Brush/Pattern/Gradient area of the Toolbox. Clicking on the gradient symbol in the Toolbox is an alternative way of bringing up the Gradients dialog.

- Put a gradient in a selection:
    1. Choose a gradient.
    2. With the Blend Tool click and drag with the mouse between two points of a selection.
    3. Colors will distributed perpendicularly to the direction of the drag of the mouse and according to the length of it.

Figure 1.24. How to use rapidly a gradient in a selection

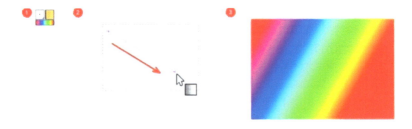

- Painting with a gradient:

    You can also use a gradient with the Pencil, Paintbrush or Airbrush tools if you choose the dynamics Color From Gradient. In the next step choose a suitable gradient from Color options and in the Fade options set the gradients length and the style of the repeating.

The following example shows the impact on the Pencil tool. You see in the upper side of the figure the necessary settings and the lower side of the figure shows the resulting succession of the gradients colors.

Figure 1.25. How to use rapidly a gradient with a drawing tool

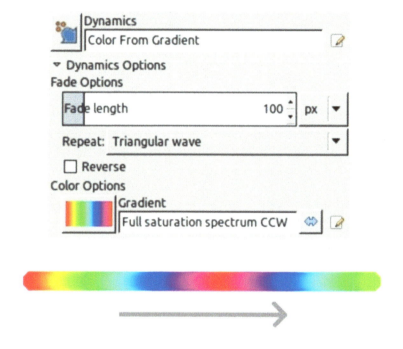

To use the Paint tools with the same settings as they were known as option Use color from gradient in GIMP up to version 2.6 open the **Tool Presets Dialog**. Then choose one of the items Airbrush (Color From Gradient), Paintbrush (Color From Gradient) or Pencil (Color From Gradient) from it.

- Different productions with the same gradient:

Figure 1.26. Gradient usage

Four ways of using the Tropical Colors gradient: a linear gradient fill, a shaped gradient fill, a stroke painted using colors from a gradient, and a stroke painted with a fuzzy brush then colored using the Gradient Map filter.

A few useful things to know about GIMP's gradients:

- The first four gradients in the list are special: they use the Foreground and Background colors from the Toolbox Color Area, instead of being fixed. FG to BG (RGB) is the RGB representation of the gradient from the Foreground color to the Background color in Toolbox. FG to BG (HSV counter-clockwise) represents the hue succession in Color Circle from the selected hue to 360°. FG to BG (HSV clockwise represents the hue succession in Color Circle from the selected hue to 0°. With FG to transparent, the selected hue becomes more and more transparent. You can modify these colors by using the Color Selector. Thus, by altering the foreground and background colors, you can make these gradients transition smoothly between any two colors you want.
- Gradients can involve not just color changes, but also changes in opacity. Some of the gradients are completely opaque; others

include transparent or translucent parts. When you fill or paint with a non-opaque gradient, the existing contents of the layer will show through behind it.

- You can create new *custom* gradients, using the Gradient Editor. You cannot modify the gradients that are supplied with GIMP, but you can duplicate them or create new ones, and then edit those.

The gradients that are supplied with GIMP are stored in a system gradients folder. By default, gradients that you create are stored in a folder called gradients in your personal GIMP directory. Any gradient files (ending with the extension .ggr) found in one of these folders, will automatically be loaded when you start GIMP. You can add more directories to the gradient search path, if you want to, in the Gradients tab of the **Data Folders** pages of the Preferences dialog.

New in GIMP 2.2 is the ability to load gradient files in SVG format, used by many vector graphics programs. To make GIMP load an SVG gradient file, all you need to do is place it in the gradients folder of your personal GIMP directory, or any other folder in your gradient search path.

 Tip

You can find a large number of interesting SVG gradients on the web, in particular at OpenClipArt Gradients OPENCLIPART-GRADIENT. You won't be able to see what these gradients look like unless your browser supports SVG, but that won't prevent you from downloading them.

Section 11: Patterns

A *pattern* is an image, usually small, used for filling regions by *tiling*, that is, by placing copies of the pattern side by side like ceramic tiles. A pattern is said to be *tileable* if copies of it can be adjoined left-edge-to-right-edge and top-edge-to-bottom-edge without creating obvious seams. Not all useful patterns are tileable, but tileable patterns are nicest for many purposes. (A *texture*, by the way, is the same thing as a pattern.)

Figure 1.27. Pattern usage

Three ways of using the "Leopard" pattern: bucket-filling a selection, painting with the Clone tool, and stroking an elliptical selection with the pattern.

In GIMP there are three main uses for patterns:

- With the Bucket Fill tool, you can choose to fill a region with a pattern instead of a solid color.

Figure 1.28. The checked box for use a pattern

The box for pattern fill is checked and a click on the pattern shows you all patterns in grid mode.

- With the Clone tool, you can paint using a pattern, with a wide variety of paintbrush shapes.
- When you *stroke* a path or selection, you can do it with a pattern instead of a solid color. You can also use the Clone tool as your choice if you stroke the selection using a painting tool.

Tip

Note: Patterns do not need to be opaque. If you fill or paint using a pattern with translucent or transparent areas, then the previous contents of the area will show through from behind it. This is one of many ways of doing "overlays" in GIMP.

When you install GIMP, it comes presupplied with a few dozen patterns, which seem to have been chosen more or less randomly. You can also add new patterns, either ones you create yourself, or ones you download from the vast number available online.

GIMP's *current pattern*, used in most pattern-related operations, is shown in the Brush/Pattern/Gradient area of the Toolbox. Clicking on the pattern symbol brings up the **Patterns dialog**, which allows you to select a different pattern. You can also access the Patterns dialog by menu, or dock it so that it is present continuously.

To add a new pattern to the collection, so that it shows up in the Patterns dialog, you need to save it in a format GIMP can use, in a folder included in GIMP's pattern search path. There are several file formats you can use for patterns:

PAT

> The .pat format is used for patterns which were created specifically for GIMP. You can convert any image into a .pat file by opening it in GIMP and then saving it using a file name ending in .pat.

> **Caution**

> Do not confuse GIMP-generated .pat files with files created by other programs (e.g. Photoshop) – after all, .pat is just a part of an (arbitrary) file name.

> (However, GIMP *does* support Photoshop .pat files until a certain version.)

PNG, JPEG, BMP, GIF, TIFF

> Since GIMP 2.2 you can use .png, .jpg, .bmp, .gif, or .tiff files as patterns.

To make a pattern available, you place it in one of the folders in GIMP's pattern search path. By default, the pattern search path includes two folders, the system patterns folder, which you should not use or alter, and the patterns folder inside your personal GIMP directory. You can add new folders to the pattern search path using the **Pattern Folders** page of the Preferences dialog. Any PAT file (or, in GIMP 2.2, any of the other acceptable formats) included in a folder in the pattern search path will show up in the Patterns dialog the next time you start GIMP.

There are countless ways of creating interesting patterns in GIMP, using the wide variety of available tools and filters -- particularly the rendering filters. You can find tutorials for this in many locations, including the GIMP home page [GIMP]. Some of the filters have options that allows you to make their results tileable.

Figure 1.29. Pattern script examples

Examples of patterns created using six of the Pattern Script-Fu's that come with GIMP. Default settings were used for everything except size. (From left to right: 3D Truchet; Camouflage; Flatland; Land; Render Map; Swirly)

Also of interest are a set of pattern-generating scripts that come with GIMP: you can find them in the menu bar, through File → Create → Patterns. Each of the scripts creates a new image filled with a particular type of pattern: a dialog pops up that allows you to set parameters controlling the details of the appearance. Some of these patterns are most useful for cutting and pasting; others serve best as bumpmaps.

Figure 1.30. How to create new patterns

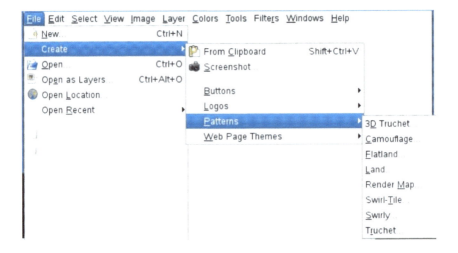

Section 12: Palettes

A *palette* is a set of discrete colors. In GIMP, palettes are used mainly for two purposes:

- They allow you to paint with a selected set of colors, in the same way an oil painter works with colors from a limited number of tubes.
- They form the colormaps of indexed images. An indexed image can use a maximum of 256 different colors, but these can be any colors. The colormap of an indexed image is called an "indexed palette" in GIMP.

Actually neither of these functions fall very much into the mainstream of GIMP usage: it is possible to do rather sophisticated things in GIMP without ever dealing with palettes. Still, they are something that an advanced user should understand, and even a less advanced user may need to think about them in some situations, as for example when working with GIF files.

Figure 1.31. The Palettes dialog

When you install GIMP, it comes supplied with several dozen predefined palettes, and you can also create new ones. Some of the predefined palettes are commonly useful, such as the "Web" palette, which contains the set of colors considered "web safe"; many of the palettes seem to have been chosen more or less whimsically. You can access all of the available palettes using the **Palettes dialog**. This is also the starting point if you want to create a new palette.

Figure 1.32. The Palette Editor

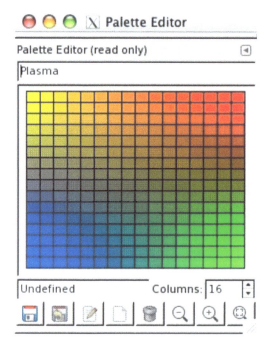

Double-clicking on a palette in the Palettes dialog brings up the Palette Editor, showing the colors from the palette you clicked on. You can use this to paint with the palette: clicking on a color sets GIMP's foreground to that color, as shown in the Color Area of the Toolbox. Holding down the **Ctrl** key while clicking, on the other hand, sets GIMP's background color to the color you click on.

You can also, as the name implies, use the Palette Editor to change the colors in a palette, so long as it is a palette that you have created yourself. You cannot edit the palettes that are supplied with GIMP; however you can duplicate them and then edit the copies.

When you create palettes using the Palette Editor, they are automatically saved as soon as you exit GIMP, in the palettes folder of your personal GIMP directory. Any palette files in this directory, or in the system palettes directory created when GIMP is installed, are automatically loaded and shown in the Palettes dialog the next time you start GIMP. You can also add other folders to the palette search path using the Palette Folders page of the Preferences dialog.

GIMP palettes are stored using a special file format, in files with the extension .gpl. It is a very simple format, and they are ASCII files, so if you happen to obtain palettes from another source, and would like to use them in GIMP, it probably won't be very hard to convert them: just take a look at any .gpl and you will see what to do.

12.1. Colormap

Confusingly, GIMP makes use of two types of palettes. The more noticeable are the type shown in the Palettes dialog: palettes that exist independently of any image. The second type, *indexed palettes*, form the colormaps of indexed images. Each indexed image has its own private indexed palette, defining the set of colors available in the image: the maximum number of colors allowed in an indexed palette is 256. These palettes are called "indexed" because each color is associated with an index number. (Actually, the colors in ordinary palettes are numbered as well, but the numbers have no functional significance.)

Figure 1.33. The Colormap dialog

The colormap of an indexed image is shown in the **Indexed Palette dialog**, which should not be confused with the Palettes dialog. The Palettes dialog shows a list of all of the palettes available; the Colormap dialog shows the colormap of the currently active image, if it is an indexed image – otherwise it shows nothing.

You can, however, create an ordinary palette from the colors in an indexed image—actually from the colors in any image. To do this, choose Import Palette from the right-click popup menu in the Palettes dialog: this pops up a dialog that gives you several options, including the option to import the palette from an image. (You can also import any of GIMP's gradients as a palette.) This possibility becomes important if you want to create a set of indexed images that all use the same set of colors.

When you convert an image into indexed mode, a major part of the process is the creation of an indexed palette for the image. Briefly, you have several methods to choose from, one of which is to use a specified palette from the Palettes dialog.

Thus, to sum up the foregoing, ordinary palettes can be turned into indexed palettes when you convert an image into indexed mode; indexed palettes can be turned into ordinary palettes by importing them into the Palettes dialog.

Figure 1.34. Colormap dialog (1) and Palette dialog (2)

Section 13: Presets

If you often use tools with particular settings, presets are for you. You can save these settings and get them back when you want.

Paint tools, which are normally in Toolbox, have a preset system that have been much improved with GIMP-2.8. Color tools (except Posterize and Desaturate), which are not normally in Toolbox, have their own preset system.

Four buttons at the bottom of all tools options dialogs allow you to save, restore, delete or reset presets.

Section 14: Drawing Simple Objects

In this section, you will learn how to create simple objects in GIMP. It's pretty easy once you figure out how to do it. GIMP provides a huge set of **Tools** and Shortcuts which most new users get lost in.

14.1. Drawing a Straight Line

Let's begin by painting a straight line. The easiest way to create a straight line is by using your favorite **brush tool,** the mouse and the keyboard.

Procedure 1.1. Drawing a Straight Line

1. **Figure 1.35. A new image**

   The dialog shows a new image, filled with a white background.

   Create a new image. Select your favorite brush tool or use the pencil, if in doubt. Select a foreground color, but be sure that the foreground and background colors are different.

2. **Figure 1.36. The start of the straight line**

The dialog shows a new image, with the first dot which indicates the start of the straight line. The dot has a black foreground color.

Create a starting point by clicking on the image display area with the left mouse button. Your canvas should look similar to *"Figure 1.35, "A new image"*.

3. **Figure 1.37. The helpline**

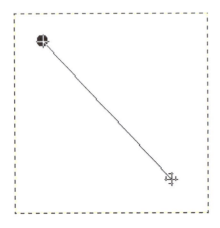

The screenshot shows the helpline, which indicates how the finished line will look.

Now, hold down the **Shift** button on your keyboard and move the mouse away from the starting point you created. You'll see a thin line indicating how the line will look.

4. **Figure 1.38. The line after the second click**

The line created appears in the image window after drawing the second point (or end point), while the **Shift** key is still pressed.

If you're satisfied with the direction and length of the line, click the left mouse button again to finish the line. The GIMP displays a straight line now. If the line doesn't appear, check the foreground and background colors and be sure that you kept the **Shift** key pressed while painting. You can keep creating lines by continuing to hold the **Shift** key and creating additional end points.

1. GIMP is not designed to be used for drawing.[4] However, you may create shapes by either painting them using the technique described in **page 67 "Drawing a Straight Line"** or by using the selection tools. Of course, there are various other ways to paint a shape, but we'll stick to the easiest ones here. So, create a new image and check that the foreground and background colors are different.

2. **Figure 1.39. Creating a rectangular selection**

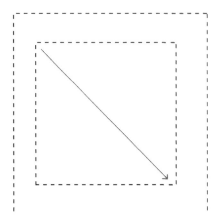

The screenshot shows how a rectangular selection is created. Press and hold the left mouse button while you move the mouse in the direction of the red arrow.

Basic shapes like rectangles or ellipses, can be created using the selection tools. This tutorial uses a rectangular selection as an example. So, choose the rectangular selection tool and create a new selection: press and hold the left mouse button while you move the mouse to another position in the image (illustrated in **Figure 1.39, "Creating a rectangular selection"**). The selection is created when you release the mouse button.

3. **Figure 1.40. Rectangular selection filled with foreground color**

The screenshot shows a rectangular selection filled with the foreground color.

After creating the selection, you can either create a filled or an outlined shape with the foreground color of your choice. If you go for the first option, choose a foreground color and fill the selection with the bucket fill tool. If you choose the latter option, create an outline by using theStroke selection menu item from the Edit menu. If you're satisfied with the result, remove the selection.

HOW TO GET YOUR COPY OF OUR 939-PAGE FULL COLOR GIMP BOOK.

First, we thank you for choosing GIMP 2.8 because if you didn't there won't be any need for a book like this.

Send an email to *contactucabelbooks@gmail.com* for a copy of the 939-page full color GIMP book.

We will appreciate it if you review this book.

Thank you.

Other GIMP Books by U. C-Abel Books

1. GIMP 2.8 Shortcuts
   ISBN-13: 978-1979461191

2. Brighter Days with GIMP 2.8   - Part I & II
   ISBN-13: 978-1517337179

3. Common Tasks in GIMP 2.8 (Full Colour) - Part I
   ISBN-13:978-1981102341

4. Becoming a GIMP Wizard   - Part II
   ISBN-13: 978-1981117208

To have a complete GIMP guide, here is what you should buy:

1. Common Tasks in GIMP 2.8 (Full Colour) - Part I
   ISBN-13:978-1981102341

2. Becoming a GIMP Wizard   - Part II

   And request for the free 939 pages book   - Part III

OR

1. Brighter Days with GIMP 2.8   - Part I & II
   ISBN-13: 978-1517337179

   And request for the free 939 pages book   - Part III